On Bended Knee

50 WAYS TO POP THE QUESTION

by Saundra Greer

Co-written and illustrated by Bill Greer

JMP

JORMAX PUBLISHING, INC.

Bloomington, Minnesota

While all stories in this book are based on successful real-life proposals of marriage, Jormax Publishing, Inc. assumes no liability for the result of YOUR marriage proposal. The experiences contained herein are intended for amusement and to provoke ideas.

Library of Congress Catalog Number: 95-079875

Printed in the United States of America.
99 98 97 96 95   7 6 5 4 3 2 1

Published by Jormax Publishing, Inc., 1620 West 98th Street, #201-202, Bloomington, MN 55431

Cover and Interior Design by Bill Greer

Dedication

My book is dedicated to my son, Bill,

who always showed me how to follow my dreams.

Also, to my wonderful granddaughters, Molly Beth and Alison Jane,

whose proposal stories I'd love to be around to hear someday.

— Saundra Greer

Contents

5□ WAYS TO POP THE QUESTION

1. Stuffed Animals
2. Las Vegas Magic
3. Slipping Into Slippers
4. The Rubber Duckie
5. Socks
6. The Photographer
7. The Jewelry Store
8. The Elegant Dinner
9. The Neat Freak
10. The Runner
11. Treasure Hunt
12. The Subway
13. Ice Cream Treat
14. Popcorn
15. The Flower Shop
16. The Picnic
17. School Projects

18. Tennis Love
19. Dropping Hints
20. Pool Diving
21. The Cleaners
22. Advertising
23. The Engraved Plate
24. The Shower Ring
25. Jewelry Box
26. Taped Message
27. Video Tape
28. The Theatre
29. Shopping
30. The Jewelry Cleaner
31. Glamour Photos
32. The "Faith" Diamond
33. The Loose Diamond
34. The Movies

35. Piggy Bank
36. On Bended Knee
37. Santa Claus
38. The Bouquet Toss
39. The Pineapple Pizza
40. The Cookie Jar
41. Shopping in Mexico
42. The Family's Blessing
43. The Basketball Game
44. The School Carnival
45. The Hand Model
46. The Ski Lift
47. Skaters
48. Leap Year
49. Skywriting
50. The Maternity Ward
51. Bonus Quickies

Preface

"What's the ring worth?"

Unfortunately, gentlemen, a few women are more concerned with the value of the diamond than they are with your feelings. They insist on knowing what the stone is worth and whether it is real. Questions like those sure put us jewelers on the spot. Although we attempt to be discreet, we cannot lie to the customer. (We do, however, wonder how our customer came to choose this woman to spend his life with). Remember, it's not the size of the diamond or its cost—the feelings of love are what matter. And, of course, so does the presentation. Show your personality, as well as an understanding of your lover's personality. Have fun (don't be nervous). The true value will be in making your proposal special and memorable. These stories are excerpts from my journal of favorite customers' schemes. Enjoy.

1.

Stuffed Animals

Jane & Jim

Jane loved stuffed animals and had quite a collection all around her apartment. Knowing this, Jim bought a stuffed kangaroo for her. Inside of the kangaroo's pouch was a baby kangaroo, and inside the little one's pouch, Jim carefully concealed a diamond ring. When Jim walked in with the toy Jane was happy enough, but upon closer examination of the lump in her kangaroo's pouch, Jane discovered the small white jeweler's box. She was ecstatic.

2.

Las Vegas Magic

Richard & Barbara

$\mathcal{B}$arb and Richard had spent a lot of time planning their trip to Las Vegas, and were very excited to finally be on their way. The flight attendant had finished the preflight announcements and the plane was ready to leave. Once again the flight attendant could be heard over the speaker, but this time it had nothing to do with flight safety. What the passengers heard now was a love limerick that ended with: "...will Barbara please be my wife?" Richard slipped the ring on Barbara's finger and the rest of the passengers and flight crew applauded! Barbara and Richard were married that weekend in a Las Vegas wedding chapel!

3.

Slipping Into Slippers

Sally & Jim

$\mathcal{S}$ally liked to be comfortable. Every day after work, she put on a pair of oversize shaggy slippers. Jim used this knowledge to plan his strategy. On this particular night, Sally got home, kicked off her shoes and headed for those slippers. While trying to get them on, she noticed something jammed in one of the toes. Reaching in to remove the obstruction, Sally discovered the diamond engagement ring Jim had put there, wrapped in foil. Sally slid the ring on her finger and accepted the proposal with tears in her eyes and slippers on her feet.

4.

The Rubber Duckie

Todd & Laurie

*E*very time Laurie took a bubble bath, she had to have her rubber duckie soap dish floating in the water. Todd arrived home early one night and prepared a special surprise for Laurie. He attached a diamond ring around the little duck's neck with rubber bands, filled the tub, added bubbles and tossed the soap dish into the water. Once Laurie was in the tub, Todd waited outside the bathroom door. It took time for the bubbles to go down, but finally Laurie reached for the soap and found a beautiful square cut diamond ring! Todd proposed tub-side; the bath was forgotten as Laurie accepted the proposal with delight.

5.

Socks

Rob & Josie

$\mathcal{R}$ob was very particular about the way his socks were put away. They had to be rolled up in a certain way, sorted into colors and put in the drawer just so. Josie and Rob had been together for a number of years, and Josie decided it was time that SHE proposed. Josie bought a wedding band for Rob and hid it in a pair of blue socks. That night they were going to a school play. Josie suggested that Rob wear his favorite blue jacket, knowing that he would need to wear his blue socks. When Rob unrolled the socks, the ring fell out. Rob was so pleased, he decided that Josie should have a matching ring. They both came into the store the next day to purchase Josie's ring.

6.

The Photographer

Sue & Peter

*P*eter, a photographer, had just gotten a ring for Sue and couldn't wait to give it to her. Sue, however was at work. Peter couldn't think about working, so he decided to propose to Sue from his office. He took a large, close-up photograph of the ring and wrote out an endearing proposal, which he then faxed to Sue's office. When Sue saw the picture and read the message, she took the rest of the day off and headed over to Peter's studio pronto. Sue accepted the proposal in person to claim the real ring, and kidnapped her fiancé for the rest of the day.

7.

The Jewelry Store

Richard & Alison

$\mathcal{I}$'ve always felt like a bit player when a young man buys a ring for his lady; this time I got to be a major part of the act. Richard had purchased a diamond ring for his girlfriend that morning. He had asked if we, at the store, would help him by putting the ring in the display window along with his proposal. Being a hopeless romantic, I agreed. That evening the couple were in the mall, window shopping. When they got to our store, his young lady, Alison, easily spotted the ring in the display case bearing the little flag that said "Will Alison marry Richard?" She was speechless for a time, but as Richard led her into the store and we fitted her ring, she alternated between laughter and tears of joy.

8.

The Elegant Dinner

Tom & Susan

$\mathcal{T}$he elegant restaurant Tom had in mind was perfect for a romantic rendezvous. The atmosphere was quiet and classy, the food deliciously prepared and kept warm under silver covers. The lovers lingered over their meal, enjoying each other's company as well as the food. Finally it was time for dessert. When the waiter lifted the cover from the plater, instead of a piece of Key Lime pie, there sat a gorgeous diamond ring. Upon leaving the restaurant, the hostess asked if everything was all right. Susan grinned and remarked that it was the best dessert she had ever had.

9.

The Neat Freak

Robert & Beth

$\mathscr{R}$obert had very definite ideas about how he wanted things to be done, and he never did anything in a small way. When it came time to propose to Beth, it was no different. Robert spent one whole Sunday wrapping the ring he had purchased in layers of bubble wrap, butcher paper, and boxes. There was no way to guess what was inside. He shipped the now rather large box to Beth via overnight express. Opening the box, Beth found a note which read "Marriage is no small matter", and proceeded to carefully unwrap the package, still thinking she'd received a large gift. Encased in all this packing material she found a small black felt box, and realized what was going on. She called Robert to give him a very definite "Yes" as she opened the ring box.

10.

The Runner

John & Mary

$\mathcal{T}$his was a tough one, unless running happens to be your sport. John, an ultra-marathon runner, had Mary, his long-time girlfriend, waiting to give him water at each rest point along the race course. As he passed one of the stops, he tossed a soggy, knotted-up handkerchief to her. While passing he said, "If the answer is yes, tell me at the next stop." She opened the handkerchief and found a diamond ring. She was so excited that she locked her keys in the car and almost had to enter the race to catch up to him! She did finally manage to get to the next stop in time to give him the affirmative answer, but John knew from a distance because he saw her smile shining from the crowd as he approached.

11.

Treasure Hunt

Ernesto & Pamela

$\mathcal{T}$his particular gentleman, Ernesto, loved playing games, and the longer the better. He proposed first, but decided to send his girlfriend Pamela on a scavenger hunt to find her ring. When she opened her appointment book first thing in the morning, she found her first clue. The clues continued to pop up everywhere during the course of the day: in her coffee cup, on her dashboard, in her coat pocket. It took the entire day, but Pamela persevered until at last the ring was found. She claimed it was all worthwhile because she had the last laugh. She told Ernesto she hadn't found the ring, and kept him going for another whole day before she said "yes!"

12.

The Subway

Scott & Joan

$\mathcal{S}$cott and Joan both usually took the same subway home each night. They rarely saw each other until they arrived at the stop. This particular day was near Christmas and the subway station was busier than usual. Scott had purchased a diamond ring that day and couldn't wait to give it to Joan. He spotted her some distance down the crowded platform— he knew it was Joan by the funny red hat she wore. Scott asked the man next to him if he would pass a scribbled message to the woman in the red tasseled hat. The message was passed on down the line until it was given to Joan— "Will you marry me? –Scott." Joan turned to find Scott waving his hands above the crowd, and she shouted "YES! YES! YES!" All the commuters were very pleased to participate.

13.

Ice Cream Treat

Mary & Don

$\mathcal{D}$on knew that Mary was very weight-conscious and that she allowed herself only one ice cream treat per month. The treat was always a huge hot fudge sundae with a cherry on top. This month Don patiently waited for the craving to overcome her. He made sure that Mary had an extra special treat. There, on top of her sundae, instead of a cherry, sat a diamond ring. She spooned it up off the top of the sundae just as if it were the cherry, and licked the chocolate fudge clean. Don rinsed it before slipping it on her finger, and they both quietly grinned and slowly finished their ice cream treat.

14.

Popcorn

David & Denise

*D*avid knew that each night before bed, Denise relaxed in front of the television with a bowl of popcorn. When she was ready to turn in, she would take the cushions off the sofa to check for stray kernels. Knowing her routine, David planted a surprise under the cushions. Denise had finished her popcorn and, as usual, taken off the cushions to brush clean underneath. There among the fallen kernels sat a diamond ring with a string tied to it. Denise followed the string underneath another cushion, where it was tied to a key to David's house and a little photo of him. What a great surprise—it was just waiting to be claimed.

15.

The Flower Shop

Holly & L.J.

*W*omen sending flowers to men has become quite popular recently. Holly had purchased a wedding band for her boyfriend, L.J. She went to a friend's flower shop and had her deliver the ring in a florist's box instead of roses. The ring was carefully wrapped in the paper lining the box. Holly included a card which read, "Roses are red, violets are blue, marry me and I'll always be true." The proposal and ring were accepted, and the couple started their happily-ever-after.

16.

The Picnic

Peter & Kathie

$\mathcal{P}$eter and Kathie loved being outdoors in the summer. They especially enjoyed picnics. This particular day Peter packed the lunch; he brought wine, cheese, fruit and a few other treats. They found a perfect picnic spot by their favorite lake and unpacked the food. As Kathie unwrapped a large wedge of Swiss cheese, glimmering from deep in one of the holes in the Swiss cheese she spotted a diamond ring! Kathie not only loved the ring and the perfect day, but got a kick out of the presentation, which she claims she'd thought of first!

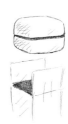

17.

School Projects

Tom & Jamie

$\mathcal{T}$om knew that Jamie always got involved with her niece's projects for school. This time her niece had to collect pop can tabs, so Jamie started saving them. Each night when her niece called for a count, Jamie dumped the jar and totalled the number of tabs. Early one morning, Tom planted a ring in the jar of tabs. This time when Jamie dumped the jar, out fell a beautiful diamond ring! This project turned out to be the commitment of a lifetime.

18.

Tennis Love

Paul & Paula

$\mathscr{P}$aul and Paula loved tennis. They played every chance they got, often at night under the lights. The first thing Paula would do is dump the canister of tennis balls courtside and stretch. This time, when she poured out the balls, a diamond ring jingled out among them, placed there by Paul earlier. This game was skipped because Paula's hands were shaking so hard that she couldn't hold the racket.

19.

Dropping Hints

Darla & Ken

$\mathcal{D}$arla really wanted Ken to buy her a diamond ring and marry her. Ken was a little older and had never been married; he seemed to be in no real hurry to change his status. Darla was beginning to get impatient and decided it wouldn't hurt to drop a few hints. She began to cut out pictures of brides and grooms from newspapers and magazines. She placed these pictures in his sock drawer, taped them to his medicine cabinet, stashed them in his briefcase...she put them everywhere. Ken eventually took the hint and proposed by cutting out a picture of a big diamond ring from a magazine ad and leaving it on her pillow. The next day they came into the jewelry store together and I sold them a ring like the one pictured in the ad.

20.

Pool Diving

Julie & James

*J*ulie had a beautiful swimming pool in her apartment complex, in which she and James spent hours together. One of their games was to drop coins to the bottom of the pool and dive for them. This day, however, instead of coins Julie saw a band of gold. When she surfaced for air, ring in hand, James swam over with a big kiss. The diamond flashed and sparkled in the water and sunshine. James said it took her 3 dives to find it—she had only been looking for coins!

21.

The Cleaners

Mel & Lissa

$\mathcal{M}$el's friend owned the neighborhood dry cleaning establishment. Mel recruited his friend to help him propose to his sweetheart, Lissa. Lissa had taken her coat in to be cleaned. Mel had his friend slip a box containing a diamond ring into the pocket. When Lissa arrived home she discovered a bulge in the pocket of her coat. Prompted by curiosity, she reached into the pocket and found the box. The ring was a perfect surprise, which she accepted with joy.

22.

Advertising

Dean & Florence

$\mathcal{T}$his gentleman, Dean, had a hard time putting his feelings into words when he was face to face with his lady, Florence. When he decided to propose, he took out an ad in the local paper. It proved easier for him to think it through and say it his own way by writing it. After she read the proposal, Florence also took out an ad to proclaim her love, and accepted the proposal for the whole city to see in the newspaper. The ring was waiting for her when she next saw her lover, Dean.

23.

The Engraved Plate

Barry & Lila

*B*arry came up with a very clever idea. He had a plate custom made with the words, "Will you marry me?" engraved on it. He had Lila over for supper that night, and served her meal on the plate. Lila was just finishing her meal when she saw the engraving. As she read it, Barry reached into his pocket for the diamond ring.

24.

The Shower Ring

Joel & Jeannie

*J*oel and Jeannie had talked of marriage many times. As they were sitting in the car, Joel jokingly pulled a shower curtain ring from his pocket and asked Jeannie to marry him. "This ring is too small for my wrist and too big for my nose," she replied. Joel then pulled a ring from his other pocket and told Jeannie that this ring should fit much better. It did indeed fit her finger perfectly.

25.

Jewelry Box

Carrie & Andrew

$\mathcal{C}$arrie loved fine jewelry and had quite a collection, which she kept in a shoe box. For her birthday, Andrew bought her a lovely jewelry box. When Carrie opened it to put away her jewels, she found a diamond ring already residing in the box. She was so busy admiring the diamond that the rest of her jewelry didn't make it into the box that night at all.

26.

The Taped Message

Betty & Ronnie

$\mathcal{B}$etty had just gotten a new answering machine. She kept trying to put a message on the tape, but it never sounded quite right. She asked Ronnie if he would please come over during his lunch hour to record some clever message for her. When Betty called home and listened to the message later in the day, she was thrilled and embarrassed that Ronnie had left her a proposal of marriage and asked that she accept the ring she would find in her top dresser drawer. Of course, anyone who called her home number also heard the message! She had a slew of messages when she got home, and a ring.

27.

The Video Tape

Susan & Bob

$\mathcal{W}$hen Susan came home from the video store where Bob worked, she inserted the tape she'd gotten into her VCR to and hit "play." The label showed the right movie, but there was a different tape playing. She watched Bob slip a gold ring on his little finger and say the ring was for her if she came back to the store. She sped back, forgetting the tape in the machine. Bob had been anxiously pacing around the video store until Susan returned.

28.

The Theatre

George & Diane

$\mathscr{G}$eorge had been carrying a ring around with him for months, just waiting for the perfect opportunity to propose. On Valentine's day Diane surprised George with tickets to a play they had both wanted to see. George seized the opportunity at the theatre and got the stage manager to help. At intermission, the master of ceremonies announced that there was a gentleman in the audience who wanted to proclaim his intentions. George stood up, took the ring from his pocket and proposed to Diane. The audience loved it, and so did Diane.

29.

Shopping

Sheila and Mark

$\mathcal{S}$heila had found "the most awesome ring" she had ever seen. She tried everything she could to get Mark to come see it. But Mark hated to shop, and would not budge. Sheila would come in and see the ring every couple of days when she was on break. All of us got to know her after a few of these visits. One day Sheila jokingly said she wished someone would call Mark and tell him how much she wanted that ring. Unbeknownst to her, I did just that. Mark decided to give in to the inevitable, and had me put the ring on his credit card. Sheila was really upset when she came in a few days later, only to find the ring had been sold. When Mark presented her with the ring, however, she was overjoyed.

30.

The Jewelry Cleaner

Steve & Beth

$\mathcal{B}$eth was very particular with her jewelry. Every day when she got home she took off all her jewelry and put it in a jar of jewelry cleaner. One morning when she took her jewelry out of the cleaning solution, she found an unfamiliar but beautiful diamond ring. Steve, in order to surprise her, had slipped the ring into the solution the night before. Beth was delighted to accept it.

31.

Glamour Photos

Bob & Rita

$\mathcal{O}$n the anniversary of the day they met, Bob gave Rita a certificate for a glamour photo session. Rita had her hair and nails done, had picked the perfect outfit, was made up and ready to go when in walked Bob. He said he had with him the only thing she was lacking to make for a perfect picture. He then presented Rita with the diamond ring she had been wanting. Other than some tear-streaked makeup that needed repair, the photo session was a great success, as was the marriage proposal.

32.

The "Faith" Diamond

Glenda & Richard

*R*ichard thought he had a foolproof idea for avoiding the expense of a diamond ring if Glenda turned down his proposal. Richard had purchased a ring with a diamond that looked convincingly real, but was not. He asked Glenda to marry him, and she said yes. The problem was, she loved the ring and Richard could not get it back—he wanted to replace the fake diamond with the real thing without letting Glenda know. Unfortunately, Glenda eventually discovered the ruse. At first she was furious, but she forgave Richard in time for the wedding .

33.

The Loose Diamond

Jessica & Jeff

$\mathcal{J}$eff was going to do everything right. He bought a loose diamond and was going to let Jessica pick out the setting if she accepted his proposal. That particular night they were going line dancing, a favorite pastime of theirs. Jeff carefully placed the loose diamond in his pocket and was ready to go. Everyone was already dancing and having a good time when they arrived on the scene, so they joined in. When Jeff popped the question later in the evening, he reached into his pocket for the gem, but it was not there! Everybody on the dance floor helped search for the loose diamond on hands and knees! It was not found. Another diamond eventually had to be purchased, but it was a memorable proposal!

34.

The Movies

Carlo & Gina

$\mathscr{C}$arlo thought he had come up with a foolproof plan to use when he proposed. Carlo took Gina to a movie, purchased some popcorn, and when she was not looking, slipped the ring into the box. Gina took a handful of popcorn and put it in her mouth. When she bit down, she bit the ring and broke her tooth. What had seemed like a good idea to start with turned into a painful experience. Gina was a good sport about it and did keep the ring (and Carlo), so all was not lost.

35.

Piggy Bank

Sonny & Roberta

$\mathcal{R}$oberta was a waitress, and saved silver coins from tips in a large piggy bank. Sonny thought it would be clever to hide a diamond ring in it and wait for the response a few days later when she counted out her change to take to the bank. But Roberta, instead of taking the money out of the pig first, took the whole thing to the bank. The piggy bank was emptied at the counter, and the ring spilled out with the rest of the coins. Sonny had been waiting for some kind of response from Roberta and was disappointed that the people at the bank enjoyed his proposal more than he, but he did wind up with Roberta.

36.

On Bended Knee

Christopher & LeeAnn

*E*ven in these modern times, the tried and true method of proposing on bended knee is still popular. To propose in this method, especially in front of witnesses, is highly romantic and respectful. It impresses not only the young lady but also mom and dad. Christopher proposed to LeeAnn at her family's reunion in this way, and it endeared him permanently to her family. The relatives still talk about it years later.

37.

Santa Claus

Jen & Rich

$\mathcal{R}$ich bought a diamond ring from me, and one day he brought his fiancée, Jen, in to meet me. I asked them how he proposed and they told me their story. A few days before Christmas, Jen and Rich were out doing some last-minute shopping. They decided to go see Santa, just for the fun of it. While standing in line, Rich told Jen he wanted to see how long it would take to reach Santa. While he was out of sight, Rich had a private talk with Santa. Jen finally sat on Santa's lap and gave him her wish list. Topping the list was a diamond ring. She was shocked when Santa pulled out a jeweler's box with a diamond engagement ring in it. She tearfully accepted the proposal in front a delighted audience of shoppers.

38.

The Bouquet Toss

Curtis & Holly

$\mathcal{C}$urtis and Holly were attending the wedding of their best friends. Curtis had already devised a plan with the bride and groom for presenting a the diamond to Holly. After the wedding and the reception came the time for the bride to toss the bouquet. Instead of tossing it randomly over her shoulder, the bride made sure that the bouquet went directly to Holly. Tied to a white rose, inside the bouquet, Holly found a beautiful diamond ring. Curtis was right behind her and proposed. The day turned out to be very special for both couples.

39.

The Pineapple Pizza

Clarence & Regina

$\mathscr{C}$larence and Regina love pizza with ham and pineapple, and order it for delivery often. On the night Clarence decided to pop the question, he ordered a pineapple pizza, and when it arrived, put the ring inside a pineapple ring. When Regina opened the box, she found her diamond sparkling among the pineapple, but didn't realize at first it was hers. She thought the pizza chef must have lost it! Clarence explained, and they both still have a good laugh every time they order a pineapple pizza.

40.

The Cookie Jar

Elaine & Rich

*E*laine and Rich had picked out a ring together, and without Elaine knowing, Rich came back one night to buy it. It was their habit to have cookies and milk each night before bed, so Rich took all the cookies out of the cookie jar and replaced them with the ring. After a relaxing evening Rich suggested that it was time for their bedtime snack. Since it was relatively early, Elaine told Rich to go ahead—she was not yet ready to settle in for bed. Finally, Elaine gave in to Rich's persuasion, and she went to get the cookies out of the jar. Elaine found the jeweler's box with the ring. It was the best bedtime treat she could have received.

41.

Shopping In Mexico

Michael & Mitzi

$\mathscr{M}$ichael and Mitzi were in Mexico on holiday. Mitzi hoped that she would get a diamond ring while on this romantic trip. While shopping one afternoon, Mitzi saw a pair of earrings in a shop window. She asked Michael to come into the store with her while she tried them on. Michael suggested instead that Mitzi go to the shop next door to get gifts for everyone at home, and he would get the earrings for her. Mitzi agreed, and wandered off to the other shop. A little later they met up, and Michael gave her the package in his hand. Thinking it was the earrings, Mitzi opened the box. There, instead of the earrings, was the diamond she had been hoping for.

42.

The Family's Blessing

Edda & George

*G*eorge had asked Edda if she wanted to pick out her own ring. Edda told George that whatever he picked out would be fine. Several months went by without the ring appearing, and Edda figured it had been forgotten. Edda's whole family was going to meet at her parents' cabin one spring weekend. Upon arrival, Edda sensed something in the air. There was a lot of giggling and whispering going on; everyone was a bit too excited, but Edda still didn't have a clue. When the family sat down to dinner, Edda's father asked George to say the blessing. At the end of the prayer, George asked Edda to marry him and slipped the diamond ring on her finger. Everyone was very pleased about the engagement, especially Edda.

43.

The Basketball Game

Linda & Anthony

*L*inda and Anthony were having a terrific time at the basketball tournament. The score was tied, and the game was going into overtime. Suddenly, "...Will Linda marry Anthony?..." was flashed up on the scoreboard. Anthony turned to Linda and handed her a small white box containing a lovely diamond engagement ring. The crowd cheered and chanted for Linda to say yes. In the excitement of the moment the crowd almost forgot about the game. It was definitely a night to remember.

44.

The School Carnival

Patsy & Harold

$\mathcal{P}$atsy and Harold were both teachers at the same school, and were helping with the annual carnival. The turnout was very good and it appeared the carnival was a big success. The day was drawing to a close, and it was time to draw names for the raffle prizes. Harold brought out a bowl filled with little slips of paper and Patsy was to draw a name. When Patsy reached into the bowl, she got not a name but a "Marry Me?" note. Harold had replaced all the name slips with proposals. In her excitement, Patsy grabbed Harold and passionately kissed him in front of the crowd. Everyone understood that to be a yes. When they stopped for air, Harold fumbled the ring out of his pocket. The students whistled and howled.

45.

The Hand Model

Tom & Paula

$\mathcal{T}$om was a professional photographer and had asked Paula to be his model. He was working for a jewelry company and needed someone to model the bracelets and rings—the only part of Paula to be seen was her hand. Toward the end of the shoot Tom brought out an exquisite diamond ring and slipped it on Paula's ring finger. She looked at the ring in awe and told Tom she wished the ring were hers. Tom said nothing at first, just finished the photo session. As he started to pack everything up, Paula told him she hated to take the ring off. Tom's reply was that it was hers to keep, if she would marry him. The picture of the ring on her finger was framed, and the ring has not left Paula's hand since that day.

46.

The Ski Lift

Jake & Annie

$\mathscr{J}$ake, Annie and a couple of their friends were taking their annual ski trip to Vail, Colorado. Jake had previously planned his presentation of the ring with his friend. While in the lift line, Jake knocked Annie's ski glove out of her hand and slipped the ring inside. His friend "found" the glove and returned it to Annie. When Annie tried to put on her glove, she discovered the ring in the finger. She screamed so loudly that the ski patrol came over, thinking Annie had been hurt. Everyone was relieved and very excited for the newly engaged couple.

47.

Skaters

Merrill & Chuck

$\mathcal{M}$errill and Chuck loved in-line skating with all their friends. Every weekend they would skate near the bandshell in the park where Caribbean steel drum music was played and people danced on wheels. Not one to stand on ceremony, Chuck convinced the musicians to play his and Merrill's favorite tune, and to stop in the middle so Chuck could propose. He prearranged for a Justice of the Peace (also on skates) to be there to marry them on the spot! They later had a more formal wedding party for non-skating friends and family, but if you were to ask them, they got engaged and married on wheels in one afternoon.

48.

Leap Year

Alice & Steve

$\mathcal{A}$lice had wanted Steve to marry her since she had met him. He loved her, but was set in his ways and slow to propose. Alice waited until Leap Year, February 29th, when it is traditionally "acceptable" for the woman to ask the man (like Sadie Hawkins Day). They had planned to go out dancing that night, and in the nightclub, on a crowded dance floor, she popped the question. He said "sure," and they danced until closing time. Steve wanted to marry on the following Leap Year, but Alice couldn't wait another four years. They wed a few months later.

49.

Skywriting

John & Lynette

$\mathcal{A}$ bit shy, but with all the right intentions, John's scheme was to propose in a big way. One day, while on John's sailboat on the lake, he asked Lynette to help him rig lines at the bow of the boat. Lynette had to grab lines from above her, so she had to look up. John had had his proposal skywritten, but the words were fading away fast—Lynette was not noticing the cloud-like "MARRY ME LYNN!" Finally, John had to point it out to her, and she snapped photos between the tears until the words faded away.

50.

The Maternity Ward (a bet)

Sandy & Jerry

*F*inally, this is how *I* received *my* ring over forty years ago. My husband, Jerry, was a friend of my cousin's. She knew he had not asked me to marry him, and he knew she didn't have any children. Every time they saw each other they would tease one another. My cousin always said, "When are you going to marry my cousin, Sandy?" My soon-to-be-husband's answer was always the same: "I'll marry your cousin when you have a baby boy." Eventually my cousin got pregnant. She had a baby boy, and I received my engagement ring right there in the middle of the maternity ward, on a bet.

51.

*Bonus Quickies**

*$\mathcal{B}$onus quickies for those of you still searching for inspiration:

- Place a ring in a wine glass (white wine only, please).

- Freeze a ring in an ice cube.

- Have the ring folded into a fortune cookie.

- Place the ring in a contact lens case.

- Conceal the ring in a box of candy.

- Use an Easter basket to present the ring.

- Bury the ring in a box of her favorite talcum powder.

- A sugar bowl is a nice place to find a ring.

- Put the ring in a half-full can of coffee.

About the Author

*S*aundra Greer is a wife, mother (four children) and grandmother who manages a jewelry store in suburban Minneapolis. She's worked in the jewelry business for 25 years, and is as enthusiastic about jewelry and the people it has enabled her to meet as the day she started. Many of Sandy's customers become friends and loyally return to deal particularly with her. *On Bended Knee: 50 Ways to Pop the Question* is a compilation derived from her work notebooks collected over the years.

This is her first book.

How did you get engaged?

Let's hear your story.

It may be included in my next book!

Saundra Greer
c/o Jormax Publishing, Inc.
1620 West 98th Street, #202
Bloomington, MN 55431

or e.mail: gemsandy@aol.com